Animals, Animals!

DO WHALES HAVE WHISKERS?

A Question and Answer Book about Animal Body Parts

by

Emily James

CAPSTONE PRESS
a capstone imprint

A+ Books are published by Capstone Press,
1710 Roe Crest Drive, North Mankato, Minnesota 56003
www.mycapstone.com

Library of Congress Cataloging-in-Publication Data
Names: James, Emily, 1983–author.
Title: Do whales have whiskers? : a question and answer book about animal
   body parts / by Emily James.
Description: North Mankato, Minnesota : Capstone Press, [2017] | Series: A+
   books. Animals, animals! | Audience: Ages 4-8. | Audience: K to grade 3.
   | Includes bibliographical references and index.
Identifiers: LCCN 2016005325| ISBN 9781515726647 (library binding) | ISBN
   9781515726685 (paperback) | ISBN 9781515726722 (eBook PDF)
Subjects: LCSH: Animals--Juvenile literature. | Anatomy,
   Comparative–Juvenile literature. | Children's questions and answers.
Classification: LCC QL49 .J26 2017 | DDC 591.4–dc23
LC record available at http://lccn.loc.gov/2016005325

EDITORIAL CREDITS:
Jaclyn Jaycox, editor; Juliette Peters, designer;
Jo Miller, media researcher; Laura Manthe, production specialist

PHOTO CREDITS
Newscom: imageBROKER/Bernd Zoller, 14; Shutterstock/Alberto Loyo, 1, back cover, Artush, 22,
Audrey Snider-Bell, 10, Eric Isselee, 28 (bottom), Erwin Niemand, 32, Ethan Daniels, 26, JGA, 16,
jurra8, 4, Lightspring, 27 (top), Mr. SUTTIPON YAKHAM, 28 (top), Neil Burton, 18, Ondrej Prosicky, 8,
Roobcio, cover, Sari ONeal, 20, Steve Byland, 24, stockphoto mania, 27 (bottom), Vladimir Melnik, 12,
Wang LiQiang, 6

Design Elements
Shutterstock: Nebojsa Kontic, Olegusk

NOTE TO PARENTS, TEACHERS, AND LIBRARIANS:
This Animals, Animals! book uses full-color images and a nonfiction format to introduce the concept
of animal body parts. *Do Whales Have Whiskers?* is designed to be read aloud to a pre-reader or to
be read independently by an early reader. Images help listeners and early readers understand the text
and concepts discussed. The book encourages further learning by including the following sections:
Glossary, Critical Thinking Using the Common Core, Read More, Internet Sites, and Index. Early
readers may need assistance using these features.

Printed in China.
007722

DO WHALES HAVE WHISKERS?

No! Seals have whiskers.

whiskers

Seals have long, wavy whiskers. Their sensitive whiskers can feel vibrations in the water. The vibrations tell the seals the size and shape of other animals in the water.

DO WHALES HAVE BEAKS?

No! Parrots have beaks.

beak

Parrots have sharp, curved beaks. Their powerful beaks can break open the hard shells of seeds and nuts. Parrots' beaks can be very colorful. Sometimes they are bright red or flaming orange.

DO WHALES HAVE FEATHERS?

No! Owls have feathers.

Owls have soft, fluffy feathers. Special feathers soften the swooping sound of the owl's wings. Hunting owls can fly silently through the forest and sneak up on their prey.

DO WHALES HAVE LEGS?

No! Centipedes have legs.

Centipedes crawl quickly, searching for food at night. A centipede's body is divided into parts. Each part has a pair of long, skinny legs. Centipedes can have as many as 177 pairs of legs.

DO WHALES HAVE TUSKS?

No! Walruses have tusks.

tusks

A heavy walrus glides gracefully underwater.
But it isn't so easy for the walrus to climb out.
The walrus uses its long, sharp tusks to pull
its big body up onto an ice floe.

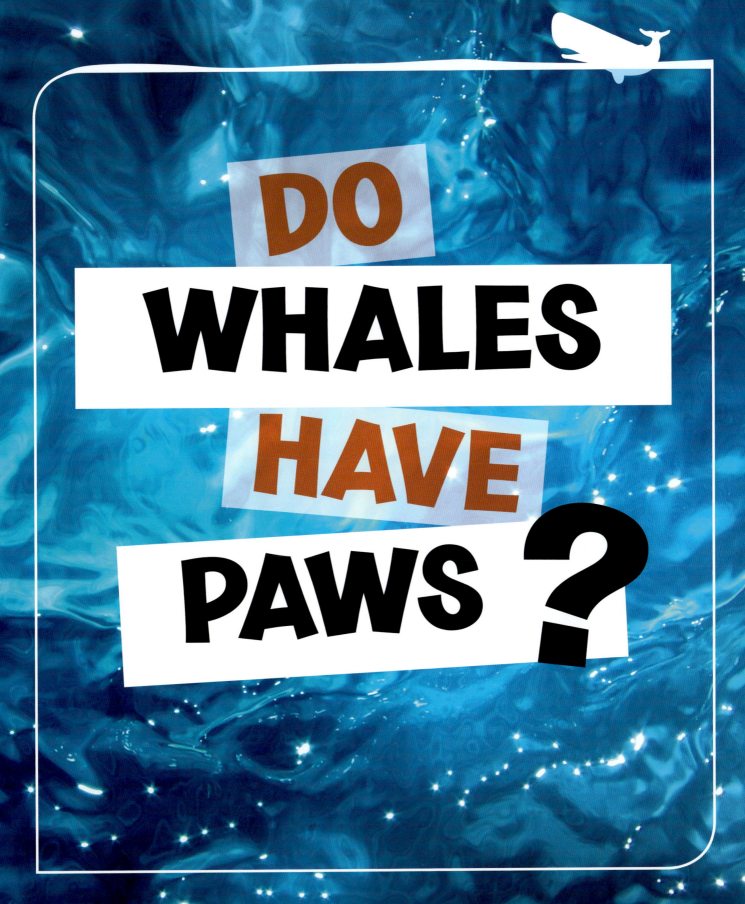

DO WHALES HAVE PAWS?

No! Puppies have paws.

Puppies with big paws often grow into large dogs. Dogs that pull sleds in the snow have very furry paws. These sled dogs often wear soft booties to protect their paws from ice and snow.

DO WHALES HAVE CLAWS?

No! Lobsters have claws.

claws

Lobsters crawl on the floor of the ocean, waving their heavy claws. One claw is strong enough to crush a crab shell. The other claw has sharp teeth that can tear the crabmeat.

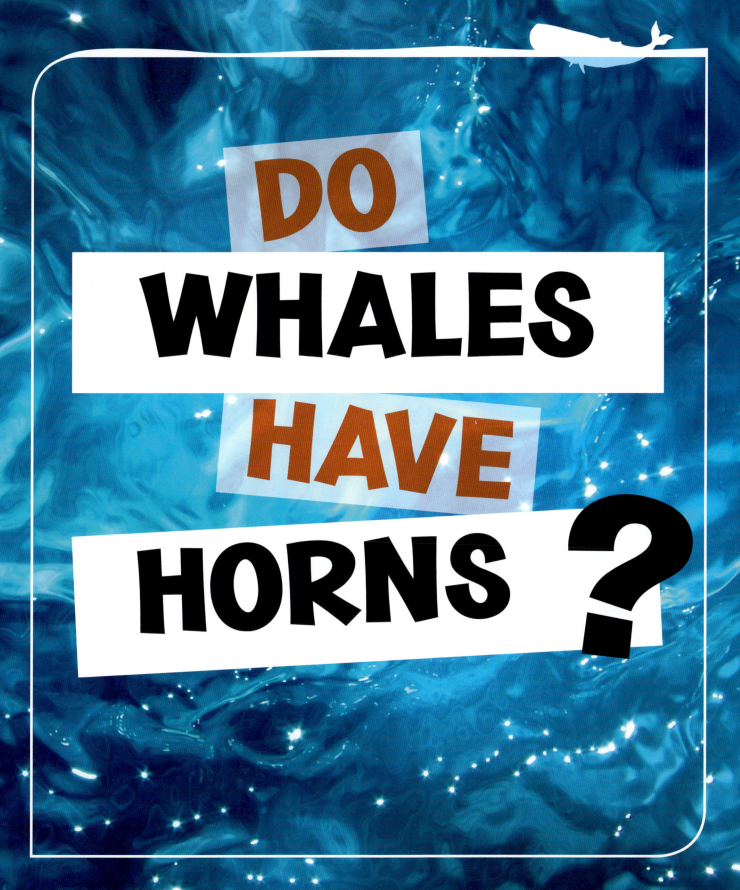

DO WHALES HAVE HORNS?

No! Bulls have horns.

horns

Bulls grow hard, heavy horns on the tops of their heads. A bull's horns are longer and sharper than a cow's horns. As a bull grows bigger, its horns curve and spread apart.

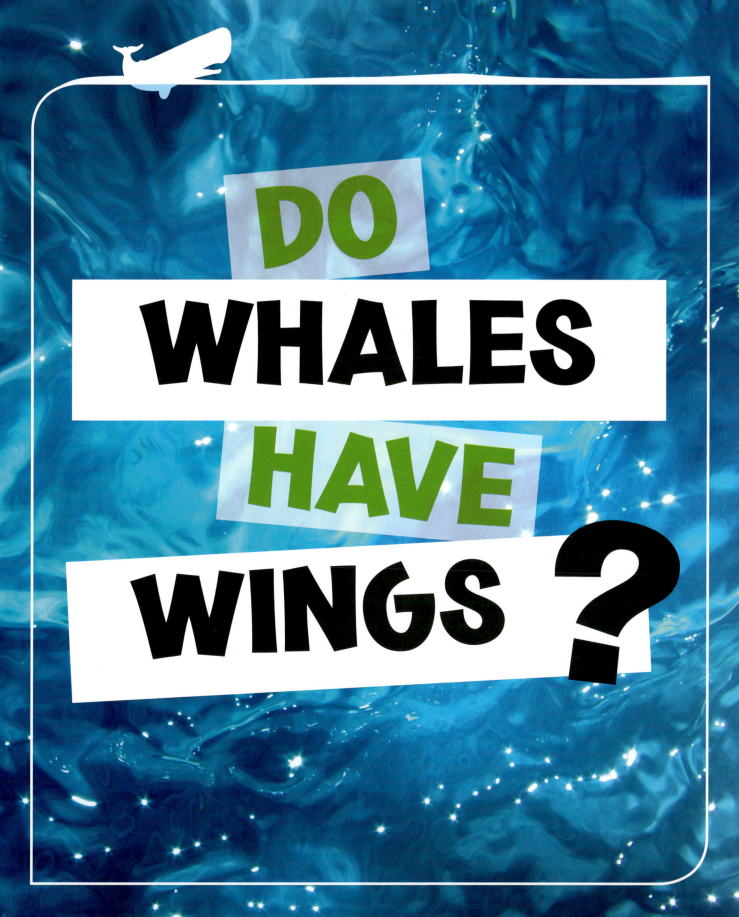

DO WHALES HAVE WINGS?

No! Butterflies have wings.

veins

Monarch butterflies have four strong wings that flutter and flap. Thick, black veins keep their orange wings stiff. These butterflies fly thousands of miles to be in a warm place for the winter.

DO WHALES HAVE TRUNKS?

No! Elephants have trunks.

trunk

An elephant's long trunk is much more than a nose. Elephants suck water into their trunks. They blow it into their mouths to drink. Elephants also use their trunks to gather food and greet each other.

DO WHALES HAVE SHELLS?

No! Turtles have shells.

shell

A turtle has a hard shell around most of its body. The shell acts like a shield and protects a turtle from predators. Many turtles can hide their heads and legs inside their shells.

DO WHALES HAVE FINS?

Yes! Whales have fins.

fluke

flipper

Whales have fins and flippers for turning and splashing. They have flukes on their tails for zooming along, leaving bubbly trails.

Animal Bodies

Some animals have bright, colorful bodies.

brilliant wings   ⟶   monarch butterflies

flashing beaks   ⟶   parrots

monarch butterfly

Some animals have bodies that blend in with their surroundings.

dark as deep water   ⟶   walruses

walrus

turtle

Some animals have hard bodies.

thick shells   ⟶   lobsters
crunchy skin   ⟶   centipedes
strong frame   ⟶   turtles

Some animals have soft bodies.

smooth, hairy skin   ⟶   bulls
fuzzy fur   ⟶   puppies
fluffy feathers   ⟶   owls
waterproof coat   ⟶   seals

Some animals' bodies are too big to hide!

heavy hulks   ⟶   whales
giant creatures   ⟶   elephants

owl

GLOSSARY

beak—the hard, front part of a bird's mouth

fin—a flap sticking out from the back of the bodies of some whales; whales use their fins for moving steadily through water

flipper—a wide, flat flap sticking out from the side of a whale's body that it uses for swimming and steering

floe—a large sheet of floating ice

fluke—the wide, flat end of a whale's tail

predator—an animal that hunts other animals for food

prey—an animal that is hunted by another animal for food

protect—to keep safe

shield—an object that gives protection from harm

stiff—hard to bend or turn

tusk—one of two very long, pointed teeth that curve out of the mouths of some animals such as a walrus

vein—a small, stiff tube that helps a butterfly wing keep its shape

vibration—a fast movement back and forth

whale—a large animal that lives in the ocean; a whale looks like a fish but is actually a mammal that breathes air

CRITICAL THINKING USING THE COMMON CORE

1. How many wings does a monarch butterfly have? What color are they? (Key Ideas and Details)

2. Turtles have hard shells that help keep them safe from predators. What is a predator? (Craft and Structure)

3. Name one body part you have. What does it help you do? (Integration of Knowledge and Ideas)

READ MORE

Lewis, Clare. *Mammal Body Parts.* Animal Body Parts. Chicago, Illinois: Heinemann Raintree, 2016.

Spilsbury, Louise. *Animal Bodies: Extreme Anatomies.* Extreme Biology. New York: Gareth Stevens Publishing, 2015.

Stewart, Melissa. *Fantastic Feet Up Close.* Animal Bodies Up Close. Berkeley Heights, NJ: Enslow Elementary, 2012.

INTERNET SITES

FactHound offers a safe, fun way to find Internet sites related to this book. All of the sites on FactHound have been researched by our staff.

Here's all you do:

Visit *www.facthound.com*

Type in this code: 9781515726647

 Check out projects, games and lots more at
www.capstonekids.com

LOOK FOR ALL THE BOOKS IN THE SERIES

DO COWS HAVE KITTENS?
A Question and Answer Book about Animal Babies

DO GOLDFISH FLY?
A Question and Answer Book about Animal Movements

DO MONKEYS EAT MARSHMALLOWS?
A Question and Answer Book about Animal Diets

DO WHALES HAVE WHISKERS?
A Question and Answer Book about Animal Body Parts

INDEX

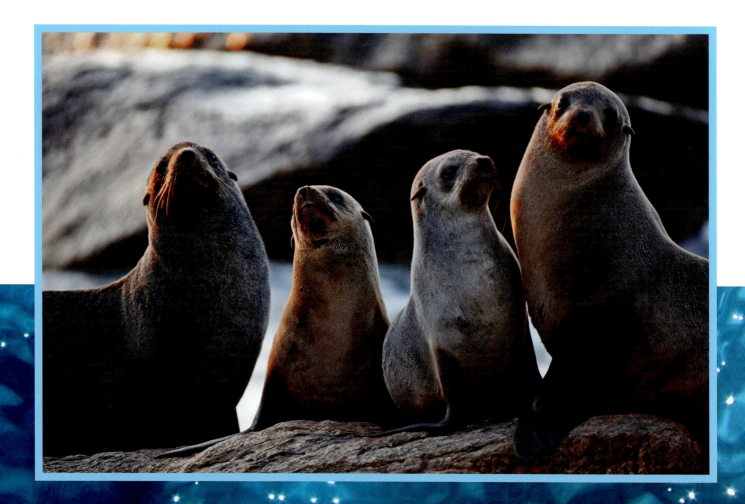